The Kattenho

WERNER DÜRRSON

———

translated by
MICHAEL HAMBURGER

THE
KATTENHORN
SILENCE

Cloudforms Number 10

Cloudforms are published by CLOUD
48 Biddlestone Road, Heaton
Newcastle upon Tyne NE6 5SL
England

Series Editor: Michael Thorp

German edition originally published by
Drumlin Verlag GmbH, Weingarten 1984

This translation has been financed by
the Förderkreis deutscher Schriftsteller in
Baden-Württemberg e. V. with support from
the Ministerium für Familie, Frauen, Weiterbildung
und Kunst Baden-Württemberg

ISBN 0 9514457 9 0

Typography by Roger and Janet Hall, Eire
Printed by Tyneside Free Press

Acknowledgements

Some of Michael Hamburger's translations from *Das Kattenhorner Schweigen* have previously appeared in *Agenda* and *Lines Review*, to whose editors grateful acknowledgement is made.

Thanks are due to John Ahouse, and particularly to Dorothea Miehe, for their linguistic assistance in the preparation of this book, and as always, to Frances.

Inhalt

Contents

Foreword

In the sequence *The Kattenhorn Silence* (which — I hope it isn't noticeable — took me years of effort to produce) I have attempted to defend myself against a too-beautiful landscape I had dreamt of since my childhood and later come to live in. The longer I lived in it, the more it threatened to silence me — by a process partly due to its gentle climate, partly to a deprivation and withdrawal: visibly nature was being replaced by building-up and specious prettification.

Kattenhorn, originally a fishing village, lies at the western end of Lake Constance, on the Höri peninsula, facing Switzerland, at the Rhine's mouth. It was in this idyll, where Vertumnus, the god of the seasons, and Pomona, the goddess of fruit-growing, exercised their peaceable dominion, that a few writers, in flight from the cities, had settled in the first half of this century, Hermann Hesse (my literary mentor) foremost among them. Later, already under pressure of the Third Reich and the Second World War, painters like Otto Dix and Erich Heckel took refuge on the remote Höri peninsula.

Perhaps I was the last poet to live there. In *The Kattenhorn Silence* the predominant element of nature and the seasons, interwoven with a love motif, confronts the inroads of modern society and politics. What remains, once again, is the poem. Since writing it — I couldn't bring myself to conduct my search for footprints under concrete — I've ceased to feel that I belong there, and can only return there in a detached way as a guest. I no longer ask myself: is it possible to stay in a place once the long-familiar has grown strange to one? I see the 'new homeland' in its density as an obstacle in the way of my necessary detachment; and cling to the experience of having glimpsed the vanishing end of a paradise that could sustain nature and human life.

WERNER DÜRRSON

Will einer wohnen,
So sei es an Treppen,
Und wo ein Häuslein hinabhängt,
Am Wasser halte dich auf.
Und was du hast, ist
Atem zu holen.

HÖLDERLIN

Quelle douceur extrême des lignes!

PAUL VALÉRY

If someone wishes to dwell,
Let it be on steps
And where a small house hangs down
Near water, there spend your days
And what is yours
Is to draw breath.

HÖLDERLIN

What an extreme loveliness of outlines!

PAUL VALÉRY

Spiegelungen

1

Untertauchen im Grünen
dachten wir, vogelleicht

katzenverschwistert, zwischen
Ufer und Schonung, Streuobst

und Wintersaat hält sich
Verstörung in Grenzen, dauert

die Liebe. Nicht schrecken
dachten wir soll uns der

Frost. Tragen das Eis.

2

See Himmel See. Milder Glanz.
Ein Hügel besänftigt den andern.
Schattenlos Licht.

Zwischen Bäumen
als Ort
ein paar Häuser am Hang.
Ohne Rauch.

Noch und noch Stille.

Hier werden
keine Kriege geschmiedet hier
wettert kein Sturm hier wiegt
was leicht ist.

Wind.

Mirrorings

1

Submerge in greenness
we thought, light as birds

siblings to cats, between
lake shore and sapling reserve

windfall and winter corn
destruction keeps within bounds,

love can last. There frost
we thought shall not

frighten, the ice support us.

2

Lake sky lake. Soft radiance.
One hill makes gentle the
other.
Shadowless light.

Between trees
for place name
a few houses on the hillside.
Without smoke.

Now and as yet stillness.

Here no
wars are assembled here
lightness preponderates.

Wind.

Im Sand
das sind nur die Spuren von
Grenzern die Spuren suchen im
Sand.

Zwei gelassene Schwäne.
Die schläfrigen Möwen.

Draußen setzen heitere Segel
Akzente.

Mir glückte zu stranden.

3

Zu spät jetzt. Hiergeblieben
sehe ich wie sich der Bach

davonläuft seewärts einem
versunkenen Himmel entgegen

den wir uns hätten an
Land ziehen können

blinkende Fische im Netz.

4

Mein Ort ist eine verlassene
Liebesgeschichte. Überwachsen die

Trampelpfade des Glücks. Der Kahn
vermodert am Grund.

Ich komme wieder, hast du
versichert, in einem Frühjahr das

immer wiederkommt hinter der Kälte
lau, mit untröstlichem Regen.

These tracks in
the sand are only the tracks of
frontier patrolmen looking
for tracks in the sand.

Two placid swans.
Those drowsy seagulls.

Outside carefree sails
set the tone.

I managed to founder.

3

Too late now. Staying
I see how the brook

runs away seaward
towards a sky that has sunk

that we could have drawn in
for us on to land

glittering in the net.

4

My place is a forsaken
love story. The beaten tracks

of luck overgrown. The dinghy
rots away in the shallows.

I shall return, you
assured me, in a springtime that

always returns after the cold
mild, with disconsolate rain.

Verbotene Gärten

1

Ihr Blumen
wo blüht ihr denn hin —

dieser Mai
ein riesiger Friedhof
mit auferstandenen Toten
als Gärtnergehilfen

wie schön *wie* heiter *wie*

echt

der Tod so bunt wie
die Hoffnung —

wer aus dem Fenster springt
fällt in die Blumen

2

Nicht dieser Forsythienschamlosigkeit
auch der weißesten
Lilie nicht

dem verkrüppelten Birnbaum aber
säße ich
gern zufüßen

spräche vertraulich
zu der zögernden Lärche

Forbidden Gardens

1

You flowers
for what, where to are you blooming —

this May
a vast graveyard
with resurrected corpses
as assistant gardeners

how lovely *how* cheering *how*

genuine

death as many-coloured
as hope —

Whoever jumps out of the window
lands in the flowers

2

At the feet not of this forsythia
shamelessness nor of the whitest
of lilies

but of this crippled peartree
I should like
to sit

and intimately speak
to the hesitant larch

griffe der sonnigen Birke
mit Schatten unter
die Arme

3

Bevor die Nacht kommt
pflanzen sie hastig in
restliche Lücken
noch Bäumchen

als ob
morgen die
Welt unterginge

lend a helping hand
with shadow
to this sun-bright birch

3

Before night falls
they hurriedly plant
more saplings
in the gaps that remain

as though
tomorrow
were the end of the world

Ins Freie

Eingeklemmt in das System
verkaufter Landschaft bleibt mir

der See noch, geh ich auf vor-
geschriebenem Weg von

Schildern belauert hangabwärts
Mauern Zäunen entlang am

Schloß vorbei komme ich zum
gefängnistorbreiten Uferstück
der Besitzlosen:

Raum der sich
auftut, befremdliche Weite

schattenlos Licht frischen
Wind um die Hüften kann ich

durch Faulschlamm durch Schlick
ins soziale'Klärwasser waten

ferne Strände vor Augen hinaus-
schwimmen bis zur Erschöpfung

Into the Open

Clamped into the system
of landscape sold off I have

only the lake left, take the pre-
scribed path

down the slope under
the surveillance of notice-boards

along walls and fences
past the castle I come to
the prison-gate-wide shore plot
for non-proprietors:

a space that
opens, alienating stretch

shadowless light fresh
breezes round my hips I can

wade through sludge and slime
into the social sewage works water

distant beaches in sight can
swim out to the point of exhaustion.

Intermezzo con moto

Lichtknall Sommer, Gebell
metallene Stimmen, ein
Lachsacklachen

die Tüchtigen kommen die
ortsbezwingenden
Herzschrittmacher, Besitzer
unsäglichen Fernblicks —

ihre Villen sind
unbesetzt
stehengeblieben aber
nicht untätig

nicht nur wuchsen im stillen
fleißig die Sträucher

Intermezzo con moto

Light bang summer, barking,
metallic voices, a
laughter bags laughter

the efficient are coming the
country-conquering
heart pacemakers, possessors
of infinite prospects —

their villas were left
unoccupied
but by no means
inactive

not only shrubs on the quiet
industriously grew

Tag und Nacht

Deine Kleider hängen
noch immer im Schrank.

Das ist ein Beweis.

Die Schuhe im Bad.
Und daß ich friere
mitten im Sommer.

Day and Night

Your dresses hang
in the wardrobe still.

That must prove something.

Shoes in the bath-tub.
And that I freeze
in the middle of summer.

Feierabend

Vogellos flirrte der Sommertag
über dem Hang. Die Landstraße kurvt
um die Hütte.

Ruhig in seinem Schatten
steht der Bauer als Baum verkrümmt
zwischen den Bäumen.

In seiner Stube wächst
Gras. Bröckeln die Wände. Dürers
abgeschnittene Hände
beten.

After Work

Birdless the summer's day whirred
over the hillside. The road bends
round the cottage.

Quiet in its shade
the smallholder gnarled as a tree
stands among trees.

In his sitting-room grass
grows. The walls crumble. Dürer's
lopped-off hands
pray.

Kein anderer Wind

Was heißt hier Entscheidungen treffen hier
weht nicht der richtige Wind
der die Bäume entwurzelt sie querlegt
Asphalt wie Fragen aufreißt die
offenstehn Dächer abdeckt

Was heißt hier sich auflehnen gegen
der kommt dir ganz lau dieser Wind der wirft
dir keine Knüppel zwischen die Beine
du kannst dich nicht gegen ihn stemmen

ganz ungerufen setzt der dich matt legt dich
sanft aufs Kreuz bevor du dagegen bist
lautloser Föhn bei erschöpfender Weitsicht oder
angewärmt aus der Richtung der Kernkraftwerke
als Fallwind immer von oben

Was heißt hier Entscheidungen treffen sich
querstellen wehren wogegen
solang hier kein anderer Wind weht kommt es
es kommt wie es muß.

No Other Wind

What here does it mean to decide here
the right wind for that does not blow
which uproots the trees lays them flat
opens asphalt like questions to
gape strips the roofs

What here does it mean to revolt against
as a breeze this wind comes to you hurls
no truncheon between your legs
you can't pit your strength against it

quite uncalled for it checkmates you
gently pins you down before you resist
soundless sirocco in exhausting visibility
warmed from the nuclear power station
a downwind always from above

What here does it mean to decide to
oppose to defend yourself from what
as long as no other wind blows here it will come
it will come as it must.

Pappelallee

Nein nichts wissen sie nichts
diese Bäume. Halten nicht Schritt
mit den Antennen.

Diese tüchtige Stämmigkeit dieses
ständige Strammstehn bestenfalls
Leisetreten und Flüstern —

        sie können nicht anders
        sagt ihr —

Nein nichts wagen sie nichts als
Standhalten blindlings. Bis sie
umgelegt werden.

. . . .

Im Fallen erschlägt wer fällt
nur selten den Fäller

Avenue of Poplars

A brainless lot quite brainless
these trees. Don't keep in step
with the aerials.

This reliable sturdiness this
constant standing to attention at best
pussyfooting and whispering —

                    They don't know better
                    you say —

A gutless lot nothing but
a blinkered steadfastness. Until
they're laid flat.

. . . .

In falling those that fall
rarely strike dead the feller

Dörfliche Kassandra

Wenn das nicht Verlaß ist.
Seit Monaten zeigt die
Uhr der Kapelle fünf
vor zwölf.

Entgegen jeder anderen
Auskunft. Jeglichem Wind.

Noch mag das zu spät sein.
Oder zu früh. Man wird sehen.

Village Cassandra

If that isn't a sure sign.
For months the
chapel clock has stood at
five to twelve.

Contrary to any other
information. To every wind.

Still that may be too late.
Or too early. We shall see.

Randerscheinungen

Wenig Mißliebiges heute außer
der Bildstörung unten links die
Abfalltüte am Wegrand.

/

Hier herrscht Ruhe. Haus
beschweigt Haus. Der Nachbar
ist unsichtbar aber
ich träume es gibt ihn.
Vom Ertrunkenen fehlt
jede Spur.

/

Föhn,
klarer als Glaube
versetzt der die Berge.
Ich greife daneben.

/

Kein nordisches Rembrandt-
Dunkel, kein Recken in
wetterleuchtende Himmel
der Hälse el Grecos.
Des Sees Verfärbungen.
Stille vor keinerlei Sturm.
Die Lage gleichbleibend
veränderlich. Mir geschieht
nichts. Es klingelt ich
zucke zusammen.

/

Marginal Details

Not much today that's amiss except
the one optical flaw down there on the left that
refuse bag on the verge

/

Peace reigns here. One house
silences the next. The neighbour's
invisible but
I dream there is one.
Of the drowned
there's no trace.

/

Sirocco,
more clearly than faith
it moves mountains.
I'm wide of the mark.

/

No northern Rembrandt-
darkness, no straining up
into lightning-bright skies
of El Greco necks.
The lake's discolourments.
Calm before no storm.
The weather remains
changeable. Nothing happens
to me. A bell rings,
I wince.

/

Sucht mich doch.
Unterzutauchen schlug ich
mich in die Büsche.
Sucht mich findet mich doch.
Schon mancher ist ertrunken
im Grünen.
Findet mich oder ich
strecke die Waffen.

/

Ach der Rhein. Kein Fluß
der Erkenntnis. Verläßt
den See, treibt fort in seine
trübste Verwirklichung.
Während der See jedem
Treibholz klarmacht
daß wer bleibt
besser wegkommt.

/

Sommers inmitten der Habewichte
bin ich der weiße Neger dem
mitgespielt wird.
Ich kann meinen Stuhl
in die Sonne stellen.
Sie mich in den Schatten.

/

Reste, ungebrochen Holunder,
Schlinggewächse aus der Molasse,
über dem Hohlweg frag ich die
Luft, wem singen die Finken
den Wind, wem neigt sich die
Weide, frage drunten den See

Look for me, then.
To submerge I
made for the bushes.
Look for me find me then.
Many a one has drowned
in greenery.
Find me or I
shall give in.

/

Ah, the Rhine. No river
of knowledge. It leaves
the lake, drifts on into
its murkiest realization.
While the lake makes
clear to each bit of flotsam
that whoever stays
is better off.

/

In summer amid the money-proud
I am the white negro who's
victimized.
I can shift my chair
into the sun.
They can shift me into the shade.

/

Residues, unbroken elder,
creeping tendrils in the molasse,
above the lane I ask the
air for whom do the finches sing,
the wind to whom does the willow
bow, ask the lake down below

wem gehören die Ufer das Wasser
und wem mein verschaukeltes
Bild drin

/

Über zurechtgestutzten Bäumen die
Avantgarde der Peitschenlampen.
Aus niedergehaltenen Sträuchern
wachsen immer mehr Schilder.
Parkplätze nur für Besitzer.
Verkehrsgefährdende Witwen.
Hoffen auf Ampeln.
Ein zurückgebliebener Maler
malt das alles noch schöner.

/

Sie tastet sich haltlos
durchs Licht, beargwöhnt
die Schatten. Den See, die
verflüssigten Grenzen
nimmt sie als Wand wahr
undurchdringlich.
Da bin ich wieder, sagt sie
zu ihrem Klavier.

/

Des Morgens die halbvertrockneten
Hieroglyphen auf der Terrasse.
Zu weit gegangen, denke ich,
trage sie flugs zurück
in die Sprachlosigkeit.

/

to whom do the banks the water belong
and to whom my rippled image
in water

/

Above trees lopped into shape the
avant-garde of the whip-lamps.
Out of hedges kept down
grow more and more signs.
Parking lots only for owners.
Widows imperilled by traffic.
They hope for traffic lights.
A painter left behind
paints it all more pretty still.

/

Unsupported she gropes her way
through the light, looks suspiciously
at the shadows. The lake, the
liquidized outlines
she sees as a wall
impenetrable.
Here I am again, she says
to her piano.

/

In the morning the half-desiccated
hieroglyphs on the terrace.
Gone too far, I think,
quickly carry them back
into speechlessness.

/

Die andere Stille.
Hinter Vorhängen
Schatten. Jemand meldet
hämmernd daß er noch
da sei. Niemand versteht.

/

Wohin bloß die Katzen verschwinden.
Droben die Aspenhofbäuerin
hat sich erhängt. *Aber*
die war krank.

/

In die Stille die mithört
zwischen Mittag und zwölf
explodierte im Birnbaum
die Elster.

/

Schlaf Kindlein schlaf
singt die Mutter im
Garten zum klickenden
Takt der Schere mit
der sie den Busch kürzt.

/

Was entflattern die Belchen.
Geschossen wird anderswo.
Hier verbluten nur Rosen,
weiß unsre Friedfertigkeit,
die nie ein Unheil ver-
schuldet hat höchstens
zugelassen.

The other silence.
Behind curtains
shadows. Someone with hammer blows
reports himself present.
Nobody understands.

/

Where do cats vanish to.
Up there at Aspen Farm
the owner has hanged herself. *But
she was ill.*

/

In the silence that listens in
between noon and twelve
in the pear-tree the magpie
exploded.

/

Sleep, my baby, sleep
the mother sings in the
garden in time with the
click of the shears with which
she is pruning a shrub.

/

Why do the coots fly off.
Shooting is done elsewhere.
Here only roses bleed to death,
so our peaceableness asserts
that never caused a
disaster but at the most
permitted it.

/

Immerzu Sonntag. Glockenpalaver.
Einst kam er herübergeschwommen
vom Bildersturm drüben:
Sankt Blasius hilf! Mir steckt
ein Wort in der Kehle.

/

(Oder wie damals drüben die
Synagoge in Flammen stand
obwohl das niemand getan hat und
die Feuerwehr kam *weil die*
glaubte es brenne richtig)

/

So
mit dem Rücken zum Landesinneren
seewärts lebend ins
Menschenleere —
Bevor deine Blicke verschwimmen
greif in die Messer des Schilfs.
Der See gibt seine Opfer
nur ungern zurück.

/

Großer Schlaf. Aber einmal im Jahr
erwachen die Geister
wirbelt der See Legenden auf
Schatten
nehmen Gestalt an mischen sich
Märtyrer Seeräuber Juden
unerkannt unter des Bischofs
närrisches Fußvolk allzeit

/

Forever it's Sunday. Palaver of bells.
Once he came swimming over
from the iconoclasm on the other side:
St. Blasius, help! A word
sticks in my throat.

/

(Or how in those years over there
the synagogue was ablaze
although no one did it and
the firemen came *because they
thought it was a real fire*)

/

So
back turned to the country's interior
living lakeward into
an absence of humans —
Before your looking blurs
clutch the blades of the rushes.
The lake is reluctant
to hand back its victims.

/

Great sleep. But once in the year
the spirits awaken
the lake stirs up legends
shadows
take shape and
martyrs pirates Jews
unrecognized mingle with
the Bishop's foolish foot soldiers

hörig hörig hörig
bis auf die Katz

/

Morgenland, über Nacht ist die
Gegend verschwunden, aus
weißen Schwaden lächeln
hohe Inseln chinesisch.
Ins Bild steigen können
bevor es entweicht.

/

Jetzt so zwischen den stummen
Blicken der Häuser. Wahrer
denke ich ist die Verlassenheit
im Gedränge, und geh in
den Wald. Einst war der
voller Umarmungen.

/

Wieder Goldruten Zinnien Phlox.
Ich bin noch immer nicht weiter.
Schon kümmert das Laub
rauchen draußen die Feuer.
Der Rüttelfalke stürzte sich
in den eigenen Schatten.

/

Klapp das Bilderbuch zu
sagt mein Kopf.
Schöner Ort für
Spaziergänge nachts.
Wenn in zahnloser Stille

at all times servile servile servile
down to the cat

/

Matutinal land, overnight the
region has vanished, out of
white scud high islands
smile Chinese.
Be able to enter that scene
before it's blotted out.

/

Now like that between the dumb
glances of houses. Truer
I think desolation is
among crowds, and go to
the wood. Once that was
full of embraces.

/

Goldenrod once again zinnia phlox.
I haven't moved on one step.
Already the leafage turns
smoke comes from windows outside.
The kestrel plunged
into his own shadow.

/

Bang your picture book shut
says my head.
A good place for
walks by night.
When in toothless silence

der Kies knirscht fortgehn
aber wohin

/

Tage wie Jahre. Damals, gestern
als sich noch krähenfreundlich
der alte Dix durch die
Gegend fluchte. Und
sie erschrak.

/

Nichts klafft nichts stößt sich
plätscherndes Wasser, vergeßliche
Schönheit. Schlaf wie
anderswo Steine. Sand. Auf
immer kürzeren Wegen immer
weniger Fragen. Efeu.

/

Im Traum, wir stehn unter Wasser,
leben bei offenen Türen Fenstern
auf du mit den Fischen, üben
tapsig die Flossenschläge der
Wortlosigkeit an schwimmenden
Tischen, der Nachbar Gold im Mund
Schlamm im Haar lädt
zu Champagner

/

Ach See du
Riesenträne der
Grundstücksmakler!

the gravel grates go away
but where to

/

Days like years. Long ago, yesterday
when still, a friend to crows,
old Dix cursed his way
through the region. And
it was startled.

/

Nothing gapes nothing clashes
lapping water, forgetful
loveliness. Sleep like
stones elsewhere. Sand. On
ways ever shorter ever
fewer questions. Ivy.

/

In dream, we stand under water,
live with open doors windows
intimate with fishes, gawkily
practise the fin thrusts of
wordlessness on floating
tables, our neighbour gold in his mouth
silt in his hair invites
us for champagne

/

Oh lake you
the estate agents'
giant tear!

/

Ehmals Kirschen und Schlehen
Korn und Mohn, zwischen
Apfelwiesen die Reben, auch
blühte die Kunst am Ufer
bevor die Umzäunungen wuchsen
Hecken nach Maß um künstliche
Gärten, Einerleirasen; Stümpfe
sprießen an begradigten Straßen
Vorfahrt, drunter röchelt
lebendig begraben
der Mühlbach

/

Hei, wie liegen wir
matt am Hang.
                    Hei
matt am Hang.
Im toten Winkel
der blüht.
            (Hinterm Berg
            hinterm Berg
brennts

/

Formerly cherries and sloes
corn and poppies between
apple meadows the grapevines, and
art blossomed, too, on the shore
before the fencing grew
hedges to measure around
artificial gardens, anyone's lawns,
stumps along straightened roads sprout
traffic signs, underneath them
buried alive
the millstream death-rattles

/

Heigh-ho, how we lie
worn-out on the bank.
                        Heigh-ho
worn-out on the bank.
In the blind angle
that flowers.
                (Behind the hill
                behind the hill
there's a fire

Paradiesisch

An Sonnenblumen könnte man
sich gewöhnen. Malwen sind selten.

Oleander Lorbeer Akazien.
Die Judeneiche. Das Rosenorchester.

Rehe bis hinter die Villen.
Hasen bisweilen. Füchse kaum noch,
Raubzeug muß man erschlagen.

Im Apfelgarten nachts Käuzchen.

Die Vögel alle. Was kichert der
Grünspecht, krächzt der Fasan.
Schnarrt das Sumpfhuhn.

Wo bleibt denn der Haubentaucher.
Der Zaunkönig sirrt. Still äugt
ein Grenzer durchs Weidengehölz.

Malwen sind selten. Brennesseln
ausgestorben. Rainfarn im
Haar macht unsichtbar.

Paradisiac

One could get used to
sunflowers. Mallows are scarce.

Oleander laurel acacia.
The Jews' oak. The rose orchestra

Deer up to behind the villas.
Hares at times. Hardly a fox left,
predators have to be slaughtered.

In the orchard at night little owls.

All those birds. What does the green
woodpecker titter for, the pheasant croak.
The moorhen rattle.

What's become of the great crested grebe.
The wren buzzes. Silently
a border guard peers through the willow scrub.

Mallows are scarce. Stinging nettles
have died out. Tansy in
your hair makes you invisible.

Tagtraum bei Föhn

Droben am Hügel lag ich zur
Traubenzeit zwischen den Quellen
und trank nicht

träumte stattdessen von dir und von
schlimmeren Gegenden —

jähes Erwachen beim Knall der
Schreckschußkanone die Schwärze
wegrauschender Stare

ein Schloß zwei Kirchen drei
Villen zufüßen wußte ich wieder
der Schrecken ist eine
Erfindung

das Schwelen verheerender Brände
ein kleines Kartoffelkrautfeuer
dort drüben

der Steckbrief ein Buchenblatt
das mir im Schlaf aufs
Gesicht fiel

Sirocco Daydream

Up on the hill I lay at
grape-time between the springs
and did not drink

dreamed instead of you and of
worse places —

woke with a start at the sound of
the scare gun the blackness
of starlings in a rush

a castle two churches three
villas below me I knew once more
that terror is an
invention

the smouldering of great conflagrations
a small potato fire
over there

the warrant of arrest a beech leaf
that fell on my face
as I slept

Kleine Wetterkunde

Viel reden hörte ich über
des Wetters Schlechtigkeit.

Wer den Regen lobte
oder Gewitter
war sofort verdächtig.

Zu schweigen von künftigem
Schnee.

Nur lähmende Schwüle blieb
unangefochten.

Dann Nebel, Blätterfall.
Frost.

Hinter Gittern
das Licht sieht
seinem Urteil entgegen.

Little Meteorology

Much talk I heard of
the weather's badness.

Anyone who praised rain
or thunderstorms
was immediately suspect.

Not to mention the prospect of
snow.

Only an enervating heat
remained beyond dispute.

Then fog, leaf-fall.
Frost.

Behind palings
the light awaits
its sentencing.

Abseits

Dann jener Herbst.
Hier fielen nur Blätter.
Anderswo Schüsse.

Bewußtloses Laub.
Ich griff in seine
Verfärbungen.

Wortlosigkeit.

Die Gräber sah ich.
Die offenen Fragen.
Zugeschüttet.

Zwischen den Fingern
rote Kassiber.
Glühende Kälte.

Der Sand an den Schuhen.

Remote

Then that Autumn.
Here only leaves fell.
Elsewhere it was shots.

Unconscious leafage.
I plunged my hand into
its discolourations.

Wordlessness.

I saw the graves.
The open questions.
Filled in.

Between my fingers
red secret messages.
A coldness that glows.

Sand on my shoes.

Der Blechschutzengel

schwirrt hinterrücks über den Hang ist
voll da fast bevor ich ihn höre
hängt über dem Garten macht Wind dröhnt
flattert sieht alles liest mit
zählt die Teller die Tassen
klirren —

so laut muß
der die Ruhe der andern vor
meiner Stille bewahren

The Tin Guardian Angel

whirrs from behind over the slope is
wholly there almost before I hear him
hangs over the garden makes wind resounds
flutters sees everything reads what I read
counts the plates the cups
clatter —

so noisily he has
to protect the peace of others
from my silence

Grenzen des Möglichen

1

Droben im Wald schön fließende Übergänge /
problemlose Pfade / du weißt nicht / sind das
schon Schweizer Bäume oder noch deutsche /

überstaatlich singen die Vögel / plätschert
der Bach / kein Reh tritt fehl /

windentlang wispern die Gräser ihr Esperanto /
fliegen die Samen / ein Grenzstein / (aha!) /
setzt europäisches Moos an / /

2

Aber was tun sie die Weltverbesserer / Denker /
Verschwörer / was tun sie — /

nehmen systembesessen die Zwänge / die Straßen
in Kauf / die Kontrollen / Maschinenpistolen und

unsere Zukunft / was tut sie — / bleibt auf der
Strecke / /

Umsonst die Lehren der Wälder / die Utopien /

vergebens sind jenseits von Ordnung und Wahnsinn
die Grenzen so schön / so fließend natürlich / /

Boundaries of the Possible

1

Beautifully up there in the forest transitions flow /
paths without problems / you don't know / are those
Swiss trees already or German trees still /

supernaturally the birds sing / the brook
plashes / no deer takes the wrong step /

downwind the grasses whisper their esperanto /
the seeds fly / a frontier post / (aha!) /
puts on European moss / /

2

But what do they do the world-improvers / thinkers /
conspirators / what do they do — /

system-obsessed they take the compulsions / the roads
into account / the controls / machine-guns and

our future / what does that do — / it remains
stuck / /

wasted the forest's lessons / the utopias /

in vain beyond order and madness
the bounderies are so beautiful / so flowingly natural / /

Schwanengesang

Verbaut ist die Ankunft der Stürme / verschüttet
die Feuerstelle / der Zorn

Schläfer zur Rechten / zur Linken / Eine Stille
wie sonst nur Diktaturen sie kennen / /

Bette sich wer kann / hier leuchten die Unter-
gänge vergoldet /

ein Landstrich geschaffen für solche / mit denen
noch Staat zu machen ist / /

Kommt nur ihr ausgedienten Verdiener / ihr abge-
schlafften Denker Dichter Anarchen / Freut euch des

Abends / hier dämmert Deutschland am schönsten / /

Swan Song

Built-up is the access of storms / bricked in
the hearth / our anger/

Sleepers right / and left / A silence/
like that otherwise known under dictatorships only / /

Let those who can make their beds / here the goings-
down, gilded, shine /

a strip of land fit for those / fit
to put up a show / /

Come on then you redundant money-makers / you done-
in thinkers poets anarchists / make the best of

evening / here most gloriously Germany dusks / /

In Baumnähe

1

Dann der Winter mit wenig Schnee
und viel Schweigen

die andere Kälte

der See geht in sich
das Wetter steht still
die Bäume geben sich schriftlich

in Zäunen verfängt sich
die Abwesenheit

2

Aber an mir
komme ich nicht vorbei

sich davonzulaufen kein
Ort kein Weg geschwind um die
Ecke zur Kneipe

ich kann mich fallen lassen
und hab mich noch immer

liegen- oder stehenbleiben
an Ort und Stelle

wenn die Baumsäge kreischt
der Schmerz in den Knochen

Near Trees

1

Then winter with little snow
and much silence

the other cold

the lake turns in on itself
the weather stands still
the trees resort to script

in fences absence
entangles itself

2

But I can't
get by my own self

run away from oneself no
place no way quick round the
corner to the pub

I can let myself drop
and still hold on to myself

lie or stand put
where I lay, stood

when the power-saw shrieks
that pain in the bones

Kleines Winterbild

Der Pfahl
am Hang

seit der Krähe
die aufflog

steht er
verlassener

Small Winter Landscape

The post
on the hillside

since that crow
flew off it

has loomed
more forsaken

Liebe winterlich

Er sei ihr kurzerhand
nachgesprungen

ein Taucher habe die Beiden
engumschlungen
am Seegrund entdeckt

hörte ich sagen

die seien selbst schuld

wo das Eis doch
so dünn war

Wintry Love

At once he had jumped in
after her

a diver had found the two
in a close embrace
on the lake bed

I heard them tell

it was their own fault

when the ice was
so very thin.

Schneefall

Nichts geht mehr.
Unbeschriebenheit.

Wo kein Ort mehr ist
komme ich mir
auf die Spur.

Sie verfolgt mich.

Snow-Fall

Nothing moves any more.
Blankness not to be filled.

Where there's no place
I track
myself down.

She pursues me.

Gefahrlosigkeit

solang der Schnee fällt
Leben stockt und
im restlichen Strauch die
Amsel nicht
zetert

wie flatterhaft aber

No Danger

as long as snow falls
life stalls and
in the residual shrub
the blackbird
does not scold

but how flighty

Seegfrörne

Als wäre es dieses abwartende Leben
verschwiegen mit frostigen Schultern und
leerem Blick seewärts

Winter für Winter vergeblich die
bessere Kälte erhoffend

das große Eis fürs Gehen Arm in Arm

Frozen Over

As though it were this life that's a waiting
speechless with frozen shoulders and
an empty gaze lakeward

Winter on winter in vain
hoping for better cold

the great ice for walking arm in arm

Jähes Erwachen

Der Hang bebt,
jähes Erwachen, hei
es geschieht was

die Aufreißer kommen die
Ausheber kommen

der Bagger mit
offenen Rachen
brüllt Guten Morgen

Sudden Awakening

The slope quakes,
sudden awakening, heigh-ho
something is happening

the rippers-up are coming the
excavators

the bulldozer with
its open maw
roars Good Morning

Lichter Moment

Gestern sah ich im See
zwischen Turm und Gemäuer
die Zukunft gespiegelt

hüpften die Blitze durch
tanzende Ebenen kochten die
Tiefen kehrte das Feuer
heim in seine Verflüssigung

alles Befestigte schwankte
stürzte zerschmolz

niemand rief oder schrie
ich stand kopf

Bright Moment

Yesterday in the lake I saw
the future mirrored
between tower and walls

lightning flashes hopped through
dancing plains deeps
seethed fire returned
home to its liquidation

all things made fast tottered
crashed down melted

no one called out or screamed
I stood on my head

Zuletzt

blieben die Äpfel an
blattlosen Bäumen hängen oder sie
lagen vollzählig im Gras.

Fürs erste wird Schnee die
Äcker bestellen. Über verwischten Zeilen
vielleicht eine Rehspur oder Striche
von Krähenflügeln

In the End

the apples remained hanging
on leafless trees or they
lay in the grass every one of them.

For the time being snow
will tend the fields. Over blurred lines
perhaps a deer's footprint or traces
of crow's wings

Biographical Note and Select Bibliography

Werner Dürrson was born in Schwenningen, in the Black Forest, in 1932, and now lives in Riedlingen/Donau. His earliest studies were in music, and subsequently in French and German literature, and the range of his work attests to a consistent awareness of the relation of the word to other media. He has made several works in co-operation with painters, and himself provided the monotypes included in the Drumlin edition of *Das Kattenhorner Schweigen*. His translations of French writing, including that of Arthur Rimbaud, René Char, and Henri Michaux, reflect a corresponding affinity with those whose work inhabits the borders of definition. His achievement has been recognised with many awards, but this is his first book to be published in England.

Schattengeschlecht (Poems, with woodcuts by Erich Heckel, Hake, Köln 1965); *Flugballade* (Poem with woodcuts by HAP Grieshaber, Hake, Köln 1966); *Wilhelm von Aquitanien Gesammelte Lieder* (Collected Songs, translations, Arche, Zürich 1969); *Mitgegangen mitgehangen* (Poems 1970-1975, Agora, Darmstadt 1975, 1982); *Schubart, Christian Friedrich Daniel* (Play, Suhrkamp, Frankfurt 1980); *Der Luftkünstler* (Stories, Keicher, Scheer 1983); *Wie ich lese?* (Aphoristic Essay, Keicher, Warmbronn 1986); *Kosmose* (Poem in Twelve Movements, Keicher, Warmbronn 1987); *Ausleben* (Poems, Elster, Baden-Baden 1988); *Werke in vier Bänden* (Poems and prose, Elster, Baden-Baden 1992).

CLOUDFORMS

A developing library of imaginative work. Urgent contemporary work interposed with that which has been allowed little or no air in the past. Work which is resonant, relevant, necessary — breathing. Each Cloudform evolves from the fullest participation of the author in visioning the whole book — aware that a book is more than a text. The reader is thus afforded the opportunity of an engagement with meaning, inclusive of human presence.

For a free copy of the current Cloudforms catalogue, with details of all titles available and those forthcoming, please write enclosing SAE to:

CLOUD
48 Biddlestone Road
Heaton
Newcastle upon Tyne NE6 5SL
England

The Kattenhorn Silence
is published in a limited edition
of 500 copies

this is copy number

149